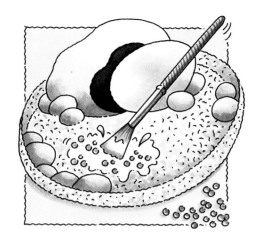

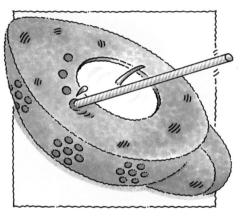

BIBLE MAKE &DO

BOOK TWO

Gillian Chapman

Craft ideas
inspired by stories
from the Bible

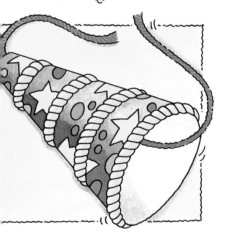
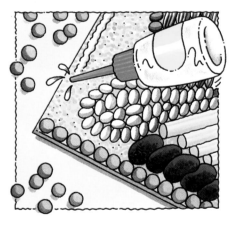

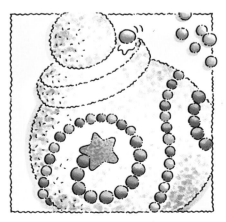

HOW TO USE THIS BOOK

You will find within this book a wealth of ideas and inspiration for using with your child, group or Key Stage 2 classes.

Discover fresh ideas for Christmas and Easter preparation, as well as bringing Old and New Testament stories to life.

Craft ideas vary from the very simple to the more challenging, but the emphasis is strongly on using inexpensive materials and equipment, recycling and using domestic materials where possible. Children will experience the thrill of making something wonderful almost 'out of nothing'.

To help keep preparation time to a minimum, each project spread features:

✷ a lively retelling of the Bible story, suitable for reading aloud to a group

✷ a list of materials needed

✷ clear step-by-step instructions

✷ a photograph of how the finished article may look, in case you haven't had time to make one earlier!

All the craft ideas have been designed, tried and tested by Gillian Chapman, a well-known author of craft books. Drawing on her experience of running children's work-shops on making books, masks and other crafts, she has prepared a helpful section of Bible Craft Tips and safety recommendations. It is worth taking a few moments to read through this section before you begin.

Part of the excitement and satisfaction of 'Make and Do' crafts begins when children are able to develop their own original slant on an idea or design, whatever the results! Some children (and adults, let's face it) may struggle to follow instructions and lose interest very quickly if they feel an activity is too difficult. Bearing that in mind, most of the ideas in this book can be modified according to a child's ability. For example, where sewing is involved, you may use PVA glue instead; where drawing is involved, you may cut pictures out of magazines.

You will find clear photocopiable tracing guides and templates in the middle of this book as a helpful starting-point. Some of these could be enlarged to produce wall-sized pictures, collages or displays for bedrooms, classrooms or churches.

Specific projects, such as masks or trumpets, could be used as props for drama productions. Having read the story and made the articles, children can enjoy the further dimension of bringing a story to life themselves through drama or dance.

There are endless possibilities for using 'Bible Make & Do' to explore the Bible. Enjoy them!

CONTENTS

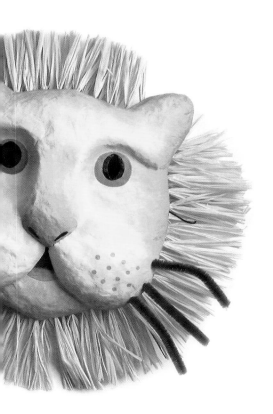

BIBLE CRAFT TIPS
Additional practical information

Safety First

All tools and equipment must be used with care and respect! Sharp pencils, scissors and needles can all be dangerous if used incorrectly...

However, an adult will need to help with carpentry tools and cutting tools.

If you need to use a craft knife make sure you also use a cutting board.

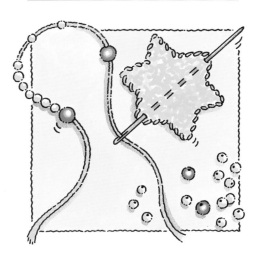

Paints

Poster paints are great for painting on paper and card, also to paint models made from paper pulp and papier mâché. They also come in metallic colours. Acrylic paints are better to paint wooden surfaces.

A jar of clean water will be needed to mix paints and to clean brushes. Change the water frequently to keep colours looking bright. Paints can be mixed on a palette or an old plate.

For detailed drawing of animals, figures and faces (as in the Noah's ark activity) sketch in the outlines first with pencil, then colour in using coloured pencils. If you have a set of watercolour paints and a fine brush use these.

Glues

PVA glue is perfect for most craftwork. It can be diluted for papier mâché type projects. It will stick paper, card and most fabrics - but in most cases it must be used very sparingly. It will wash off with cold water.

Glue sticks are better for neat finishes, but only work on paper and thin card.

When using PVA to do fine work such as gluing beads and sequins onto fabric, try to buy the glue in a bottle with a fine nozzle. If you don't have such a container then pour some of the glue into a small plastic container (like a lid) and use a cocktail stick to put tiny blobs of glue where it is needed.

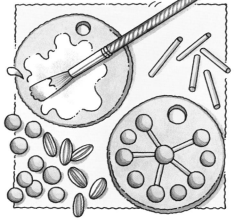

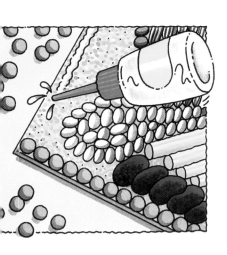

Brushes

Keep separate brushes for painting and gluing. Always clean them in warm soapy water after use and dry them before putting them away.

Keeping Clean

Make sure all work surfaces are protected with newspaper and all clothing is covered with overalls (e.g. an old shirt) or an apron. Keep an old towel handy for drying not-so-clean hands.

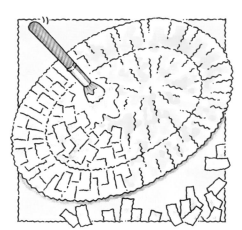

You will need:

✂

Sheet of A3
thin coloured card

Sheets of A4 thin
coloured card

Scissors

Pencil

Glue stick

Scraps of coloured paper
for decoration

NOAH'S ARK

Noah trusted God to keep him safe in the flood.

Noah was a good man, but all around him there was trouble.

God had made a wonderful world, but the people had spoilt everything.

There was fighting everywhere.

God told Noah what he planned to do. He was going to send a great flood.

God told Noah to build a boat and to fill it with two of every kind of animal on the earth.

God would keep them safe in the boat when the flood came.

Noah built a huge wooden boat called an ark. They covered it with tar to keep out the water. It would float on the waters until the flood was over.

Noah packed food for his family and all the animals.

They were ready for the day when the rain began and the rivers burst into flood.

God promised to keep them safe.

Make an ark and animal cards to help remember the story of Noah.

To make the folder, fold the sheet of A3 card in half, press firmly along the crease and open up. Take a sheet of A4 card, fold in half lengthways, open up and cut along the fold. Cut the top corners off these two strips.

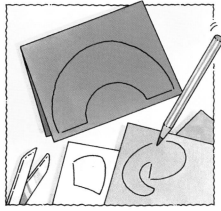

2 Use the glue stick to spread a strip of glue along the long side and bottom of the two strips and stick them to the inside of the folder, as shown.

3 Cut out shapes from the sheets of coloured papers to decorate the front of the folder. Cut out the large roof and hull shapes first and glue them in place using the glue stick. Then add any other details you wish. Don't forget to decorate the inside of the folder too.

4 To make the cards, cut a sheet of A4 card in half, then fold each piece in half. Decorate the cards with simple animal shapes cut out from the coloured papers. Start by drawing and cutting out body shapes, then heads. Place the pieces on the card first before sticking down to make sure they are the right size and check that the card folds are at the top. You can use the templates on pages 16–18 to help you.

5 Try to make the animals as colourful as possible. Cut out features, like ears, tails, tusks, spots and stripes and use the gluestick to glue them neatly into place. When all the pieces are stuck down, shape the top corners of the card and cut out the space between the legs, cutting through both sides of the card.

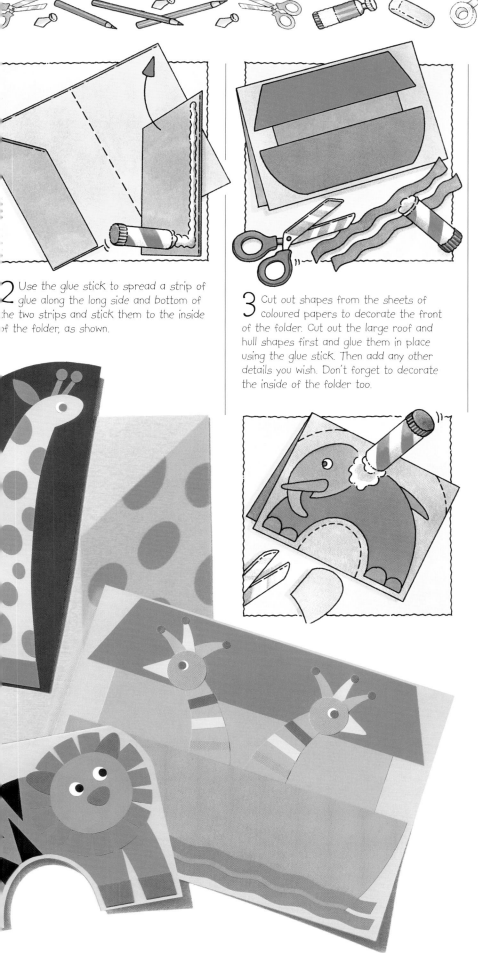

6 The tall giraffe card is made in the same way, but the fold of the card runs along the left side. Try making lots of different shaped cards. Small gift tags are made from a single thickness of card, threaded with string. Keep all your animal cards in the ark folder, so they are handy for that unexpected birthday!

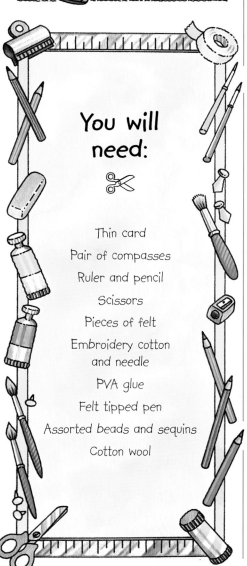

GOD'S PROMISE TO ABRAHAM

God told Abram to count the stars in the sky.

Abram was a good man who followed God. He left his home to settle in a new land which God showed him.

God promised to make Abram's family very important for many years to come. The problem was, Abram and his wife Sarai could not have children. Without children, their family could not grow any bigger.

But one day God told Abram that he would have a son and a very large family.

'Look at the stars and try to count them,' said God. 'You will have as many people in your family as the number of stars you can see.'

Imagine how amazed Abram felt about that!

Abram was now an old man and had thought he would never have any children. But he trusted God and believed his special promise.

When Abram was ninety-nine years old, God's promise started to come true!

God gave Abram a new name – Abraham. And… a new son!

You will need:

✂

Thin card

Pair of compasses

Ruler and pencil

Scissors

Pieces of felt

Embroidery cotton and needle

PVA glue

Felt tipped pen

Assorted beads and sequins

Cotton wool

Make this star mobile to help you remember God's promise to Abraham.

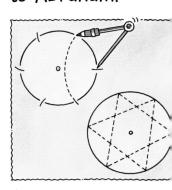

1 First, you will need to make some star templates. Use the compasses to draw a 15cm diameter circle on the card. Keeping the position of the compass points the same, use them to mark six points around the circumference of the circle. Join up these points to make a star.

2 Make two more star shapes from 10cm and 5cm diameter circles and cut them out. Use the card templates to make the felt stars. Place the template on the felt, draw around it with a felt tipped pen and cut it out with scissors. You will need 2 x 15cm stars, 6 x 10cm stars and 6 x 5cm stars.

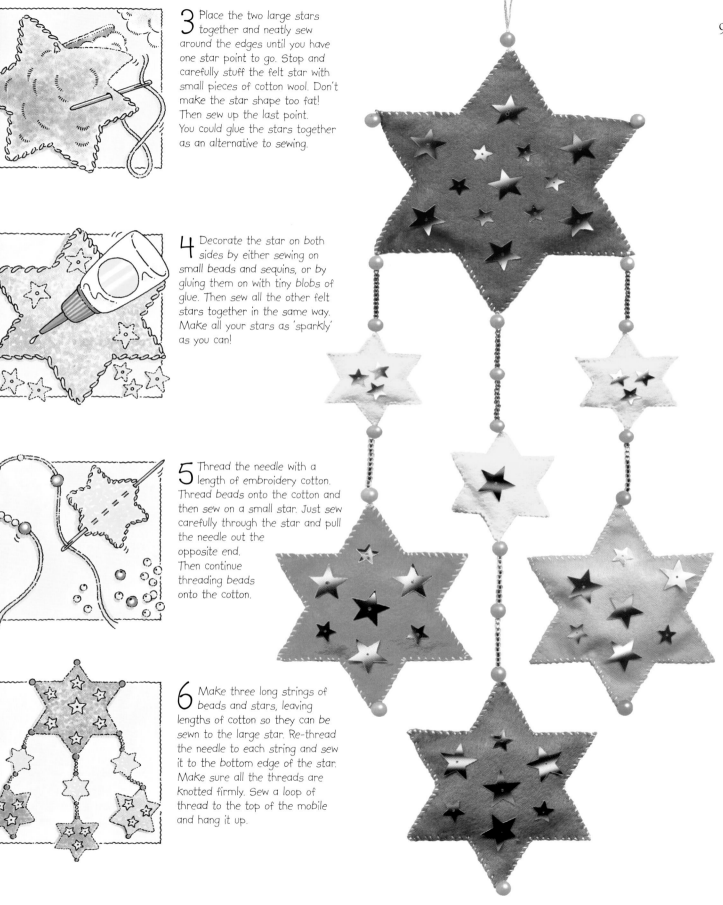

3 Place the two large stars together and neatly sew around the edges until you have one star point to go. Stop and carefully stuff the felt star with small pieces of cotton wool. Don't make the star shape too fat! Then sew up the last point. You could glue the stars together as an alternative to sewing.

4 Decorate the star on both sides by either sewing on small beads and sequins, or by gluing them on with tiny blobs of glue. Then sew all the other felt stars together in the same way. Make all your stars as 'sparkly' as you can!

5 Thread the needle with a length of embroidery cotton. Thread beads onto the cotton and then sew on a small star. Just sew carefully through the star and pull the needle out the opposite end. Then continue threading beads onto the cotton.

6 Make three long strings of beads and stars, leaving lengths of cotton so they can be sewn to the large star. Re-thread the needle to each string and sew it to the bottom edge of the star. Make sure all the threads are knotted firmly. Sew a loop of thread to the top of the mobile and hang it up.

JACOB AND ESAU
Esau is tempted by a tasty stew!

Esau and Jacob were twin brothers, but they were not at all alike.

Esau had red hair and was very hairy. He was a skilful hunter and loved being outdoors.

Jacob was a quiet man who liked staying at home. He loved cooking.

Esau was born first, which meant that when his father died, Esau would be given all that his father owned and a special blessing. Jacob secretly wanted to be the one to get this, so he planned to trick his brother.

One day, when Esau came home from hunting, he was very hungry. He could smell a delicious stew that Jacob had been cooking.

'Give me some of that stew,' he asked Jacob.

'Only if you promise to let me be the one who gets Dad's special blessing,' said Jacob.

Esau couldn't resist the stew any longer, so he promised to let Jacob have their father's blessing and all he owned. Esau only cared about his hungry tummy!

Jacob was very pleased that his trick had worked.

1 Sketch out your design on paper. Draw the stewpot and the ladle. Decorate the pot with patterns and have some steam rising out of the top. Finally draw a patterned border around your design. You can use the template on page 20.

You will need:

✂

Sketching paper and pencil

Felt tipped pen

Sheet of sandpaper and thick card

Scissors

PVA glue

Glue spreader or brush

Collage materials: dried aduki and haricot beans, lentils, green split peas, pasta shapes and sunflower seeds*.

*Please remind children that raw beans are not edible and small peas could be a choking hazard.

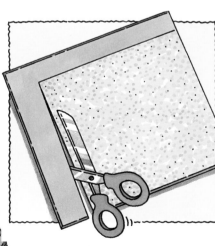

2 Use the PVA to glue the sandpaper to a sheet of thick card and leave to dry. The sandpaper will give the collage a lovely textured background. Trim the sandpaper to the same size as your design.

Make this collage stewpot and think about Jacob's trick.

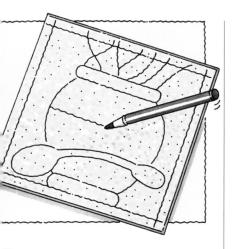

3 Following the design, sketch the outlines of the main shapes onto the sandpaper using a felt tipped pen. This will give you guidelines when you start assembling the collage.

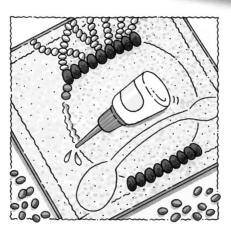

4 Begin with the main shapes. Spread the glue along the outlines and press the beans into the glue. Work around the stewpot, the lines of steam and fill in the ladle.

5 Spread PVA glue over the centre of the stewpot and fill in the shape with rows of different coloured beans and pasta shapes.

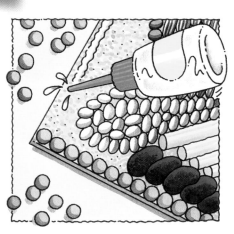

6 Spread the glue along the lines of the border pattern and press a row of beans around the edge. The PVA glue will dry clear so there shouldn't be any blobs of glue showing when it dries.

GIDEON'S VICTORY
'A sword for the Lord and for Gideon!'

Gideon was a leader in Israel. He knew that God was on his side and would help him defeat the Midianite army. He gave each soldier a trumpet and a jar with a burning torch inside.

'This is what we must do,' he told his army. 'When I get to the edge of the camp, watch me and copy what I do. When I blow my trumpet, blow yours too and shout, "A sword for the Lord and for Gideon!"'

So Gideon and his men came to the edge of the camp in the middle of the night. They blew their trumpets and broke the jars they were holding. All the other soldiers did the same.

Everyone broke their jars, picked up their trumpets and shouted: 'A sword for the Lord and for Gideon!'

The enemy army ran away! God had helped Gideon win the battle.

You will need:

✂

Sheets of thin coloured card and paper

Pencil

Clear sticky tape

Scissors

Length of thick cord

PVA glue and brush

Black felt tipped pen

Coloured string

Paints and brush, coloured stickers, stars or shapes to decorate the trumpet

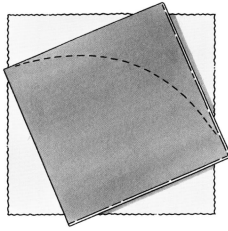

1 Take a square of coloured card and draw a curve across a corner, as shown. then cut off the excess card using the scissors.

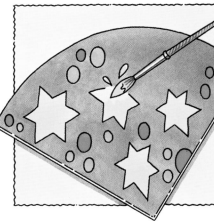

2 If you want to paint the trumpet, it is best to do it while the card is flat. You could also decorate it with coloured shapes and stars, or stickers if you have them.

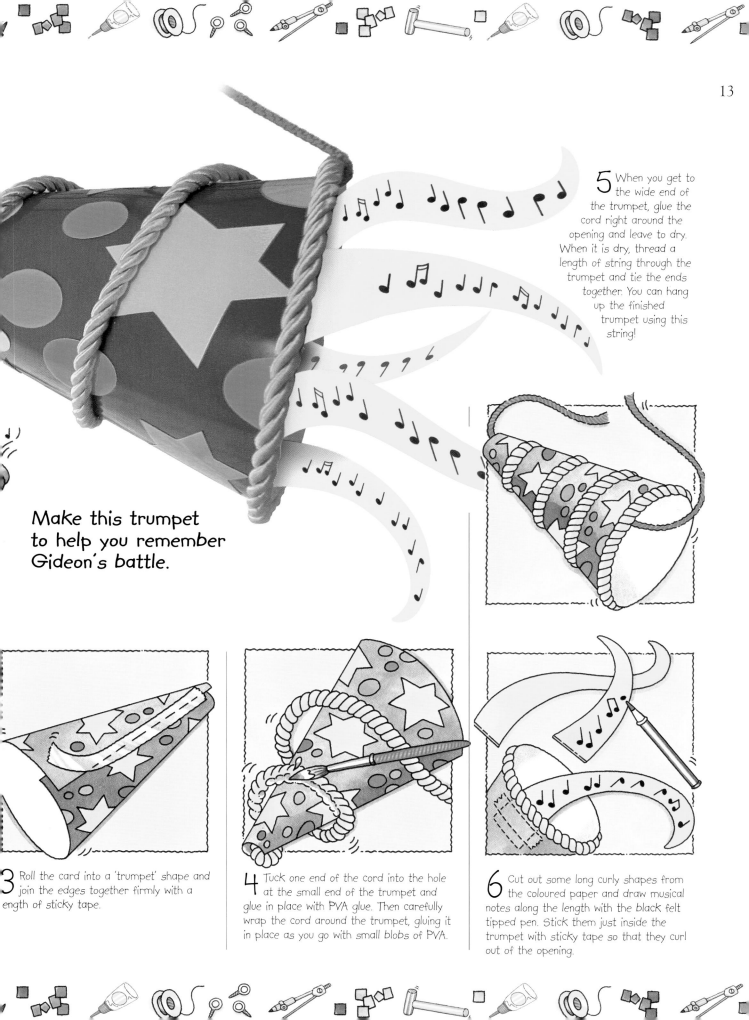

5 When you get to the wide end of the trumpet, glue the cord right around the opening and leave to dry. When it is dry, thread a length of string through the trumpet and tie the ends together. You can hang up the finished trumpet using this string!

Make this trumpet to help you remember Gideon's battle.

3 Roll the card into a 'trumpet' shape and join the edges together firmly with a length of sticky tape.

4 Tuck one end of the cord into the hole at the small end of the trumpet and glue in place with PVA glue. Then carefully wrap the cord around the trumpet, gluing it in place as you go with small blobs of PVA.

6 Cut out some long curly shapes from the coloured paper and draw musical notes along the length with the black felt tipped pen. Stick them just inside the trumpet with sticky tape so that they curl out of the opening.

DANIEL IN THE LIONS' DEN

You will need:

White sketching paper

Ruler

Rolling pin and board

Newspaper

Paints and paint brush

Raffia and large blunt needle

Length of thin elastic

Pencil

Plasticine and cutting tool/blunt knife

Cling film

PVA glue and brush

Scissors

Pipe cleaners

Daniel was thrown into a pit of lions but they didn't eat him!

Daniel was taken to live in a country far away from his home. He loved God and prayed to him, but the people around him didn't like it.

Daniel worked hard and the king made him a leader.

But Daniel's enemies were jealous and plotted against him.

The king had made a rule that no one should pray to anyone but the king for thirty days, or they would be thrown into a pit of lions. When Daniel still prayed to God, he was arrested and taken

Make this lion mask and pretend to be one of the lions in the pit.

1 First, plan the design for your lion mask.
Measure the width of your face and draw a large circle of this diameter. Add simple features: eyes, ears, nose, whiskers and mane. You can use the template on page 19.

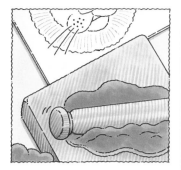

2 Looking at your sketch, make a simple plasticine mould for the papier mâché mask.
Roll out the plasticine to a thickness of 3cm. Cut out a large circle for the face, then triangles for the ears, a wedge shape for the nose, and small circles for the cheeks. Roll out 'sausage' shapes for the eyebrows.

3 Use your shapes to build up the lion's features and make a 3D mould.
Then cover the plasticine mould with cling film.

4 Tear up small strips of newspaper. Use a diluted solution of PVA glue to cover the mould with six layers of paper. Make sure each layer covers evenly.

5 Leave the mask to dry. Then carefully pull the layer of cling film away and use it to remove the mask from the mould. Trim around the mask with scissors and cut out the eye holes. Paint the lion mask.

6 Use a sharp pencil to make holes around the mask. Thread the needle with lengths of raffia and sew them through the holes. Knotting them at the back. Use the pipe cleaners for whiskers. Make two holes on each side of the mask, thread elastic through and adjust to fit.

to be fed to the lions! The king was horrified because David was his friend but he hoped that Daniel would somehow survive.

As soon as morning came, he went back to the lions' pit and called, 'Daniel! Has your God saved you?'

Daniel called back, 'Yes! I'm alive!' God had sent an angel to stop the lions from harming him.

The king released Daniel and punished the men who had tried to hurt him.

Daniel was free to pray to God for the rest of his life, and the king honoured Daniel's God who had the power to save.

TRACING GUIDES

NOAH'S
ARK
Page 6

NOAH'S
ARK
Page 6

TRACING GUIDES

NOAH'S
ARK
Page 6

DANIEL IN
THE LIONS' DEN
Page 14

TRACING GUIDES

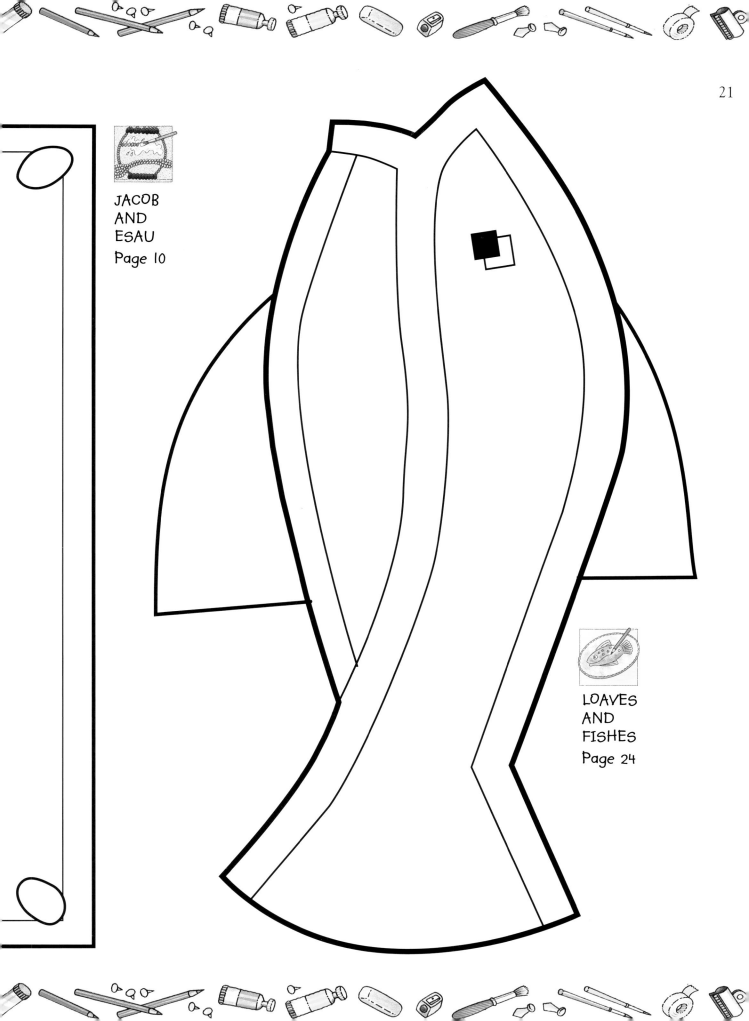

JACOB
AND
ESAU
Page 10

LOAVES
AND
FISHES
Page 24

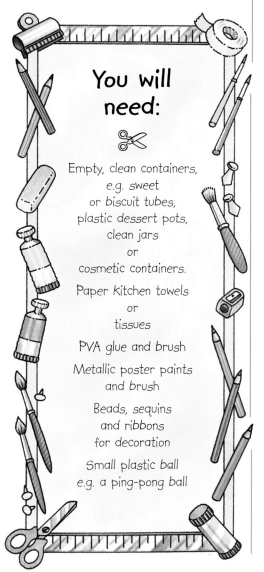

You will need:

✂

Empty, clean containers,
e.g. sweet
or biscuit tubes,
plastic dessert pots,
clean jars
or
cosmetic containers.

Paper kitchen towels
or
tissues

PVA glue and brush

Metallic poster paints
and brush

Beads, sequins
and ribbons
for decoration

Small plastic ball
e.g. a ping-pong ball

WISE MEN'S GIFTS
Wise Men followed a bright star to find Jesus.

Jesus was born in Bethlehem.
Wise Men in lands far away spotted a very bright star in the sky.
They thought it meant that a new king had been born.
So they set off and followed the star.
On their way, the Wise Men came to King Herod's palace.
'Do you know where the new king has been born?' they asked.
King Herod didn't want there to be another king in the land. He was jealous. He asked the Wise Men to find Jesus, then return and tell him.

The Wise Men followed the star all the way to Bethlehem, where they found Jesus with Mary and Joseph. They gave Jesus special gifts of gold, frankincense and myrrh.

God warned the Wise Men in a dream not to go back to King Herod, so they went home by a different road.

1 To make the round gift box, use a clean glass honey jar with a screw top lid. Remove the lid, then brush a small part of the surface with PVA glue. Begin to stick torn pieces of paper towel onto the glue, but avoid gluing paper to the screw top rim.

2 Continue to cover the surface of the jar, making sure that the paper remains nice and crinkly. Also cover the lid. When they are completely covered leave to dry, and then add on more layers to give an extra crinkly textured surface.

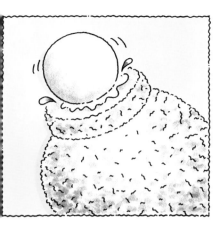

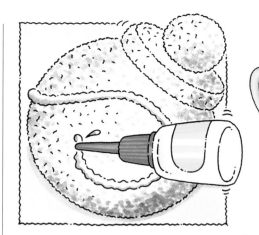

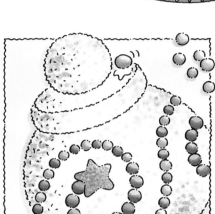

3 Glue the plastic ball to the lid and cover it with PVA glue and paper. When all the glue is dry, paint the jar and the lid with the silver poster paint.

4 Now you can decorate the jar with beads and sequins. If you have PVA glue in a bottle with a nozzle, use the nozzle to make swirly patterns on the side of the jar, or just use the glue brush to make the patterns. Then start to press the beads and sequins into the glue.

Make these gift boxes and jars and think about the special gifts given to Jesus.

5 Allow the beads and sequins on one side of the jar to dry before continuing around the other side, otherwise you may dislodge the patterns before they have the chance to dry. Don't forget to decorate the lid!

6 Create other gift boxes by using different shaped containers. Give the lids extra height and shape by sticking on small lids and bottle tops. Cover them with the glued paper, paint them with gold or copper metallic paints and decorate them with different coloured ribbons and beads.

24

LOAVES AND FISHES

Jesus feeds more than five thousand people!

Jesus was once speaking to a large crowd of people. There were men, women and even children. They had been listening to him all day and were getting hungry.

Jesus' friends thought the people should go away and buy some food, but Jesus wanted to feed them.

'What food have you got?' he asked his friends.

'Only five loaves and two fishes,' they replied.

Jesus then did something amazing! He shared out the food amongst everyone!

No one went away hungry. Jesus gave them all enough to eat, and there were twelve baskets full of left-overs.

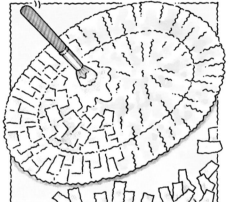

1 Use the plastic plate as a mould. Lightly grease the plate with cooking oil and cover with cling film. Then cover the plate with six layers of newspaper strips, glued with diluted PVA. This will form the plaque for your mosaic.

You will need:

✂

Oval plastic plate

Newspaper

Grey paint and paint brush

Pencil

Varnish (optional)

Cooking oil and cling film

PVA glue and brush

Scissors

Coloured magazine pictures

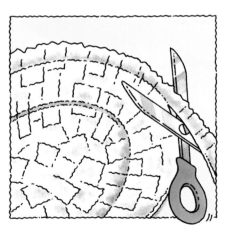

2 Leave the paper plaque to dry overnight, then remove it from the plate by pulling away the cling film. Neaten the plaque by trimming around the edge with scissors.

3 Choose a neutral grey colour to paint the plaque. This will be the base colour of your fish mosaic.

This beautiful mosaic fish will remind you of how Jesus fed the people.

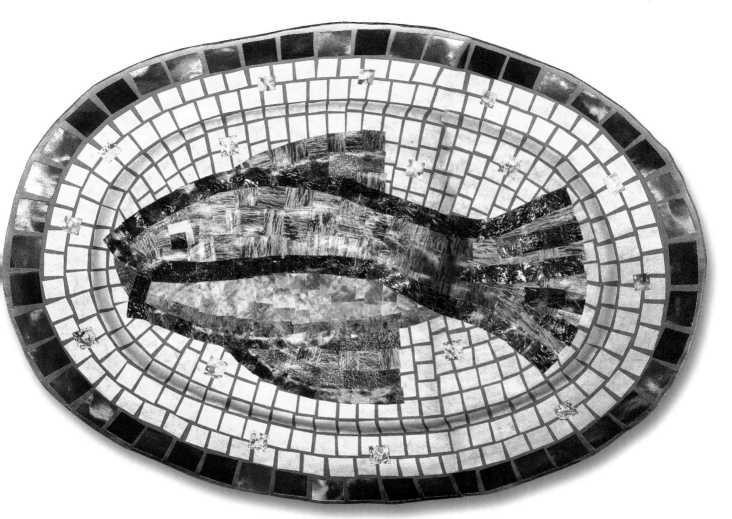

4 Sketch the outline of the fish design onto the plaque with a pencil. Add in details like the eye, fins and tail, and make a border round the edge of the plaque. You can use the template on page 21.

5 Cut out squares of coloured paper from magazine pictures. Arrange the paper squares into groups of similar colours.

6 Follow the pencil lines of the fish, and glue the squares to the plaque with PVA. Build up the mosaic pattern, overlapping the squares if necessary. Finally, you could varnish the finished plaque to strengthen and protect the mosaic.

26

THE WISE AND FOOLISH GIRLS

Five girls were ready for the wedding, but five were not!

You will need:

✂

Self-hardening clay

Night light

Plastic carving tools and plastic knife to shape and cut the clay

Small sponge and water

Paints and varnish

Jesus once told a story about ten girls at a wedding:

'There were once ten girls who were supposed to meet the bridegroom on his way to the wedding. They carried oil lamps to light the way. But the oil didn't last long in the lamps.

Five of the girls remembered to bring some extra oil with them. But the other five had forgotten. Their lamps went out and they had to run off to buy some more.

While they were away, the bridegroom arrived. The five girls whose lamps were burning brightly met him and went with him to the wedding. The door was shut.

When the other five girls finally arrived, they were too late for the wedding!'

Take a piece of self-hardening clay and knead it in your hands until it is soft. Make a circle of clay roughly 1cm thick and 10cm across. This will be the base of the lamp.

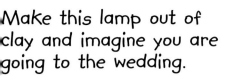

Make this lamp out of clay and imagine you are going to the wedding.

2 Place the night light in the centre of the base. Use small pieces of clay to build up the sides of the lamp, keeping the night light in place in the centre.

SAFETY NOTE:

The clay lamp is designed to hold a night light in a safe way - BUT it should not be lit without adult supervision or left unattended.

3 Mould the shape of the lamp with your fingers. Moisten the surface of the clay with a damp sponge to make it easier to work and shape.

4 Make a handle for the lamp from a piece of clay. Wet the side of the lamp and attach the handle, then smooth over the joins with the tools and the damp sponge.

5 Continue to smooth the sides and top of the lamp, using your fingers. Make the shape of a spout by pinching in the side of the lamp opposite the handle. Keeping the clay damp makes it easier to smooth the surface.

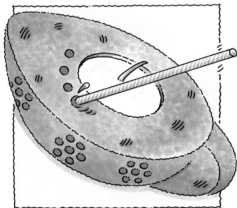

6 Make some simple patterns on the lamp using the tools and leave to dry. The lamp can be left in its natural clay finish or it could be varnished and painted.

THE LOST COIN

Jesus told this story to show how people are special to God.

You will need:

✂

Pair of compasses

Pencil

Ruler

Stiff card

Scissors

PVA glue and brush

Lengths of coloured cord or thick thread

Single hole punch

Large blunt needle

Silver poster paint and brush

Green split peas, spaghetti and sunflower seeds for decoration

Make this coin necklace with card medallions.

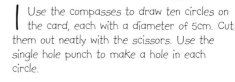

1 Use the compasses to draw ten circles on the card, each with a diameter of 5cm. Cut them out neatly with the scissors. Use the single hole punch to make a hole in each circle.

2 Brush PVA glue onto each circle and use the dried peas, seeds and pieces of spaghetti to make patterns in the centre of each circle. These shapes will make an attractive raised design on each coin, so don't worry about extra blobs of glue!

'A woman had ten silver coins.
She lost one and tried hard to find it.
She lit a lamp, swept her house and looked everywhere for it.
Suddenly she found it! There it was, glinting in the sunlight.
The woman called her friends and neighbours and said,
"Let's have a party! I am so happy to have found my lost coin!"
In the same way, God is very pleased when anybody turns to follow him.'

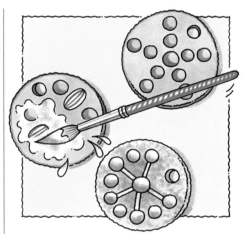

3 When all the textures are firmly glued in place and the glue is dry, paint the coins on both sides with silver poster paint and leave to dry.

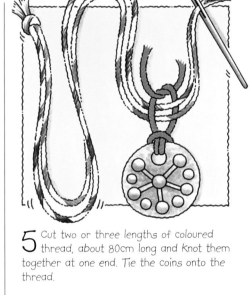

5 Cut two or three lengths of coloured thread, about 80cm long and knot them together at one end. Tie the coins onto the thread.

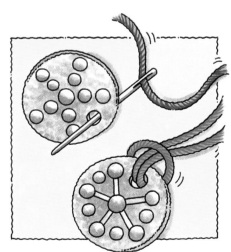

4 Thread the needle with a 12cm length of thread. Pass it through the hole in the first coin and loop the thread around the hole. Then repeat this for all ten coins.

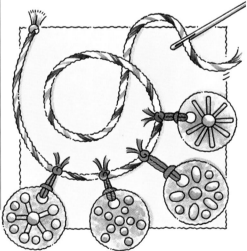

6 Place the finished necklace around your neck, tie the two ends together and cut off any surplus lengths. You could experiment by making other necklaces with lots more coins decorated with different textures.

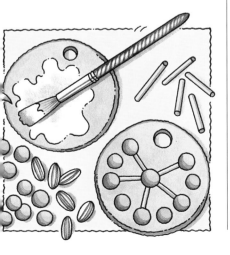

JESUS IS ALIVE!
The empty tomb.

It was three days since Jesus had died on the cross. All his friends were heart-broken and didn't know what to do next. Some of the women went to his tomb early on Sunday morning, but they had a shock! The large stone which blocked the entrance to the tomb had been rolled away!

Inside the tomb, Jesus' body had gone. All that was left were strips of cloth which the body had been wrapped in. Suddenly two men in bright shining clothes appeared.

'Don't look for Jesus here,' they said. 'He's alive!'

The women couldn't believe it! They ran home at once and told Jesus' friends.

Very soon they saw Jesus again for themselves. It was true! Jesus was alive!

You will need:

Large round lid (a lid from a large biscuit tin is ideal)

Black, brown and white poster paint and brush

Collection of small pieces of dried bark and twigs

Collection of small fresh flowers, leaves and moss

Collection of different sized stones and pebbles*

Gravel*

PVA glue and brush

Kitchen towel

* Health and safety precaution: these materials should be washed thoroughly before children handle them.

1 First you will need to disguise the shiny tin lid. Tear up small pieces of kitchen towel and glue them to the inside and rim of the lid with PVA, giving the surface a rough texture.

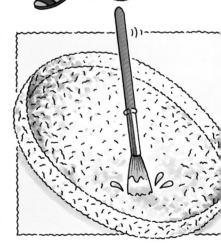

2 Make sure the shiny surface is completely covered, especially around the outside of the rim, then leave to dry. Paint the textured surface with brown and white paint, giving it a dappled finish.

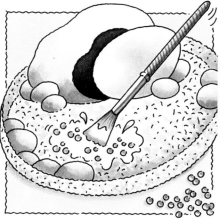

3 The largest pebble will represent the tomb. Use the black paint to paint a circular shape on the side of the pebble to represent the entrance to the tomb.

4 Position the large pebble on the lid and find another pebble to represent the stone that would have been rolled in front of the entrance hole. Glue these in place with PVA.

5 Arrange the rest of the smaller stones around the edge of the lid and next to the large pebbles and glue these in place. Then brush the inside of the lid with PVA and sprinkle gravel into the glue.

Make this miniature garden scene to show Jesus' empty tomb.

6 Place the small pieces of dried bark, twigs, small flowers, leaves and moss in your Easter garden.

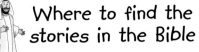

Where to find the stories in the Bible

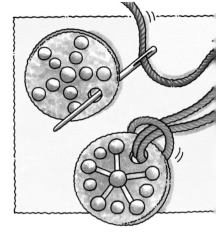

Noah's ark

Genesis 6:12 – 8:22

God's promise to Abraham

Genesis 15:1-6; 21:1-7

Jacob and Esau

Genesis 25:24-34

Gideon's victory

Judges 7:15-25

Daniel in the lions' den

Daniel 6

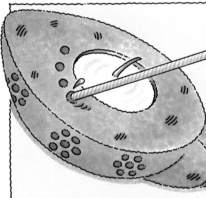

Wise Men's gifts

Matthew 2:1-12

Loaves and fishes

Matthew 14:13-21

The wise and foolish girls

Matthew 25:1-13

The lost coin

Luke 15:8-10

Jesus is alive!

Luke 24:1-12

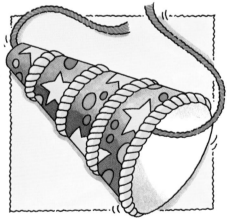

Published in the UK by
The Bible Reading Fellowship
First Floor, Elsfield Hall. 15-17 Elsfield Way,
Oxford OX2 8FG
ISBN 1 84101 333 1

First edition 2003

Editorial Director Annette Reynolds
Project Editor Leena Lane
Art Director Gerald Rogers
Pre-production Tania Jeganathan
Production Deb Greenwood and Annabelle Halliday

British Library Cataloguing in Publication Data.
A catalogue record for this book is available from
the British Library.

Printed and bound in China

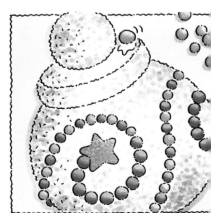